ENVIRONMENTAL SYST

CW01573088

Mediterranean Environments

D. C. Money

Evans

Evans Brothers Limited

Published by Evans Brothers Limited
Montague House, Russell Square
London WC1B 5BX

Evans Brothers (Nigeria Publishers) Limited
PMB 5164, Jericho Road, Ibadan

First published 1982

Acknowledgements
All photographs were taken by the author

Line illustrations by Reproduction Drawings

Filmset and printed by BAS Printers Limited, Over Wallop, Hampshire

ISBN 0 237 29271 8 PRA 7296

Contents

Cover photograph The olive trees rise above the brightly coloured plants of rosemary garrigue in the mountains of central Crete. Notice the effects of solution on the limestone rocks in the foreground and the accumulation of residual red soil in which the vegetation is rooted.

A Systems Approach

Here we are concerned with ecosystems and with socio-economic systems and their interactions. In a *mature* ecosystem the complex plant and animal organisms and the elements of their habitat are approximately in a state of equilibrium.

The definition and examination of systems, more or less simplified for study purposes, enables the complexities of the real, observed world to be considered in an orderly manner. We can see more clearly the interrelationships between the components of a system and the flows of energy and matter which take place within it. We simplify to see how the system is structured and to consider how the components may be further studied and measured. Simplifications involve subjective actions. It is important to define the limits of study and to specify the systems and sub-systems under consideration; and, in practice, field measurements and analysis are required to establish causal relationships between the environmental variables selected for study.

A systems approach enables us to study selected areas by isolating relevant variables in the lithosphere, atmosphere and biosphere and to consider in turn their respective influences and their combined effects. This is a helpful procedure in the case of the so-called 'Mediterranean lands'; for though they each experience typical hot, dry summers and mild winters with rain at times, and have broadly similar types of vegetation, they are widely separated globally, so that there are many floristic differences between one continental area and another. Also, in each continental region the differences in parent rocks, relief and micro-climates produce a variety of habitats, with their own particular soil conditions and plant communities—small ecosystems, whose plant–soil sub-systems we may perhaps select for special study.

The natural vegetation and soils in each of these regions have been drastically disturbed during the last hundred years or so. Before this, the extent of interference varied from one continental region to another. The aborigines of south-west Australia and the hunting and gathering Indians of California caused little permanent disturbance; nor did the nomadic Hottentots of south-west Africa, though white settlement has modified the Cape environment for over three hundred years. Central Chile, however, was farmed by Amer-Indians many centuries before the Spanish-Mestizo occupation, and the lands about the Mediterranean have experienced thousands of years of continuous settlement. Arable farming was established long before the development of the Greek city-states. By examining representative systems, we can see the consequences of disturbing established cycles between the atmosphere, soils, plants and other organisms, and so appreciate what has happened, or what may happen, in these broadly similar environments.

The Vegetation–Soil System

In any ecosystem within the broad areas shown in Fig. 4 no physical or biotic factor operates in complete independence; everything within it is related to everything else to some degree, and there are a large number of variables. Our aims are to identify the most important variables *within* the ecosystem and the extent to which particular external variables control these relationships. Here we identify a plant system and a soil system, between which are transfers of energy and materials. Plant productivity largely depends on soil nutrient inputs, so we look at the interactions of those key components which affect the available nutrient store in the soil.

Figs. 1 and 2 show an open system and the direction of exchanges of energy and matter with its environment. These are needed for its maintenance and preservation, and allow the particular soil and vegetation to reach a state where their properties appear almost constant over a long period—approaching a steady state equilibrium.

The chosen internal components are those of the plants and soil. Climatic elements are shown among the external independent variables. But climate also affects the internal variables, such as the rate of weathering of the rocks, the release of soil nutrients, losses through leaching, and saline accumulations through persistent evaporation. We shall see that climatic conditions vary considerably within each Mediterranean region, and so, therefore, does the nature of the local vegetation, though this may be influenced by factors other than climatic.

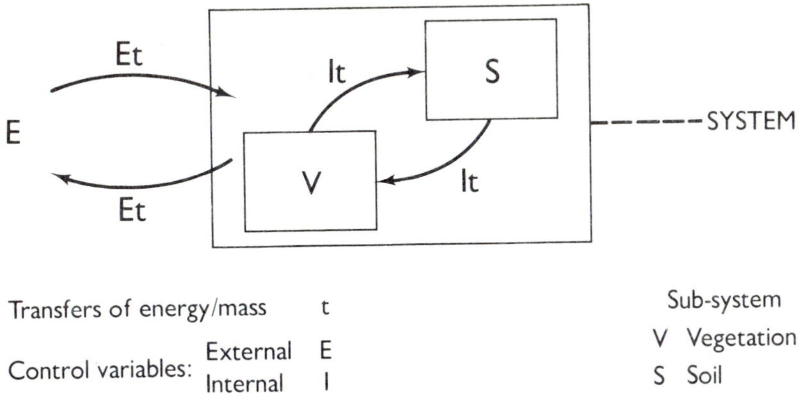

Fig. 1 A selected system with internal transfers, such as nutrient exchanges between the soil and vegetation sub-systems, and external transfers, for example solar energy inputs and transpiration losses to the atmosphere.

The Availability and Storage of Nutrients

The atmospheric elements carbon, hydrogen, oxygen and nitrogen make up 95 per cent of the dry weight of protoplasm in plants. Many other elements are needed by most living organisms, and these are made available for plants by the weathering of rocks and soil particles. Calcium, magnesium, potassium, sodium, phosphorus, sulphur, silicon, iron and aluminium are widely available—though a soil may lack a particular element. Weathering releases other elements which plants may require in very small amounts, but which are vital to their development—such as manganese, zinc, copper and cobalt.

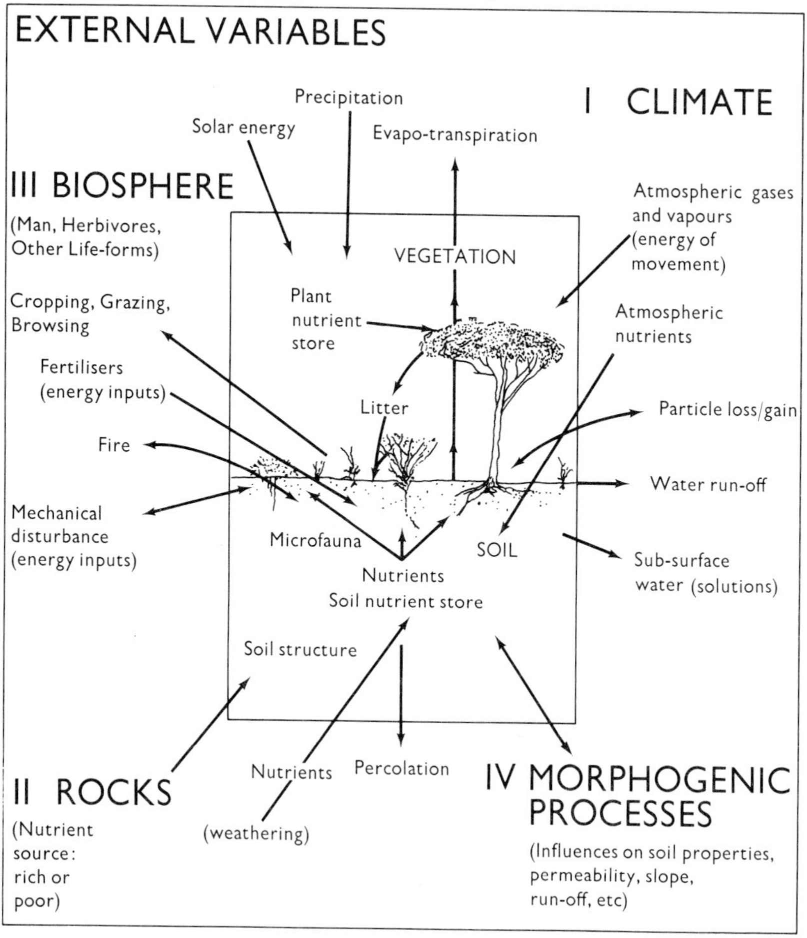

Fig. 2 Four broad categories of external variables used to enable us to look *in turn* at the influences on a given soil–vegetation system, (for example, I seasonal climatic variations, II rock weathering, III burning and grazing, IV tectonic uplift), and to appreciate their interactions.

Very soluble compounds are available for absorption by plants, but are apt to be lost from the soil by leaching. However, tiny clay particles in association with humus (as a clay–humus complex) can firmly retain vital metal ions (cations). These cations pass into the plants in exchange for hydrogen ions released from rootlets.

The nutrients released from solution are temporarily 'stored' in plants, together with the elements received from photosynthesis and nitrifying processes. They are returned to the surface as plant litter. When this decomposes, it releases them into the soil. It also provides organic acids, which may act on mineral particles and help to weather the bedrock. Soil organisms help the cycling of nutrients between plants and soil. Many of them act to break down plant litter, and nitrifying bacteria help to restore the nitrogen lost by leaching or other causes. Earthworms and other soil organisms mix the soil mineral particles and help to distribute organic matter within the soil. The nutrient content of the plant–soil system and the development of the plants themselves are, of course, affected by the rate of release of minerals from the bedrock and regolith.

In fact, man's progressive interference with the natural vegetation of the lands about the Mediterranean has disturbed both the hydrological and nutrient cycling systems. Much of the lowlands and hill slopes was once covered by evergreen mixed forest, so that soils developed in the shade of trees, which preserved relatively moist, cool ground conditions far into the summer drought. Leaf fall and decay provided much humus

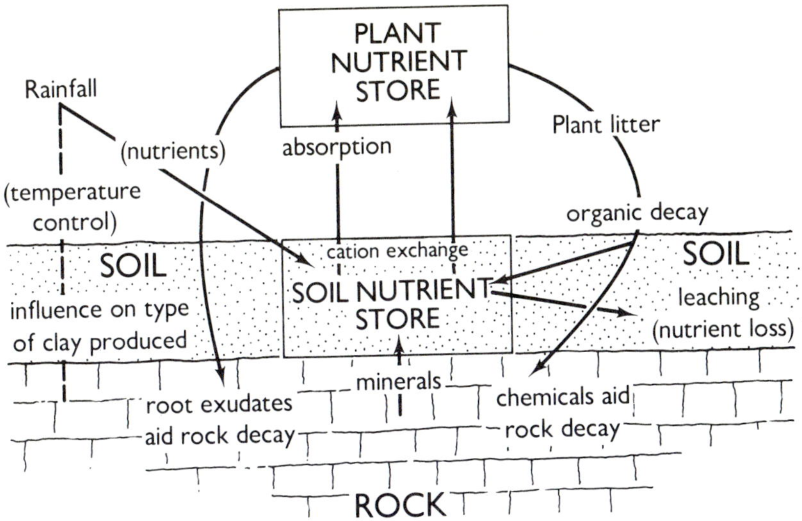

Fig. 3 A nutrient cycle, which includes some complex interactions: mineral nutrients pass from rocks to soil to plants: chemicals exuded by plant roots may accelerate rock weathering; and organic acids from litter help to break down clay particles.

for deep, brown soils, which played an essential role in the balanced cycling of nutrients between the plants and the soil. Forest clearing, burning, and grazing by man's animals exposed the top soil to the desiccating effects of summer, and allowed increased sheetflow and channelled run-off after winter storms. Deprived of abundant humus, the nature of the soils changed. The rapid removal of mineral particles by wind and water makes it difficult for mature soils to develop, especially on slopes. The characteristics of the many skeletal and residual soils of the Mediterranean lands are considered on p. 21.

Extensive forest still covers the moister parts of central Chile and south-west Australia, which have a comparable climatic regime. Yet many Mediterranean lands which receive similar precipitation now bear only a sparse shrubby vegetation. In all these countries, there are large areas of degraded vegetation on land cleared of forest.

The Location of the Mediterranean Lands

Broad Climatic Influences

Fig. 4 shows that these warm temperate lands are on the western side of the continents at about latitude 35°. They lie polewards of the world's most extensive hot deserts. In summer each experiences lengthy drought as it comes under the influence of dry subsiding air—Tc air of the tropical continental airmass which is mainly responsible for the broad arid zone. But in winter, when the source of Tc air lies nearer the equator, they also receive air from polar maritime (Pm) and polar continental (Pc) sources. The meeting and interaction of air from polar and tropical sources produces unstable conditions and stormy spells. Belts of precipitation, associated with depressions formed over the western oceans, also pass across these regions. The passage of cyclonic systems draws in air from adjoining land masses, and, in the Mediterranean especially, causes sudden temperature and moisture changes. In winter, maritime influences are particularly strong in the western parts of the Mediterranean regions, but diminish eastwards and to the lee of high relief. The continental characteristics of low precipitation and summer storms become more pronounced towards the interior.

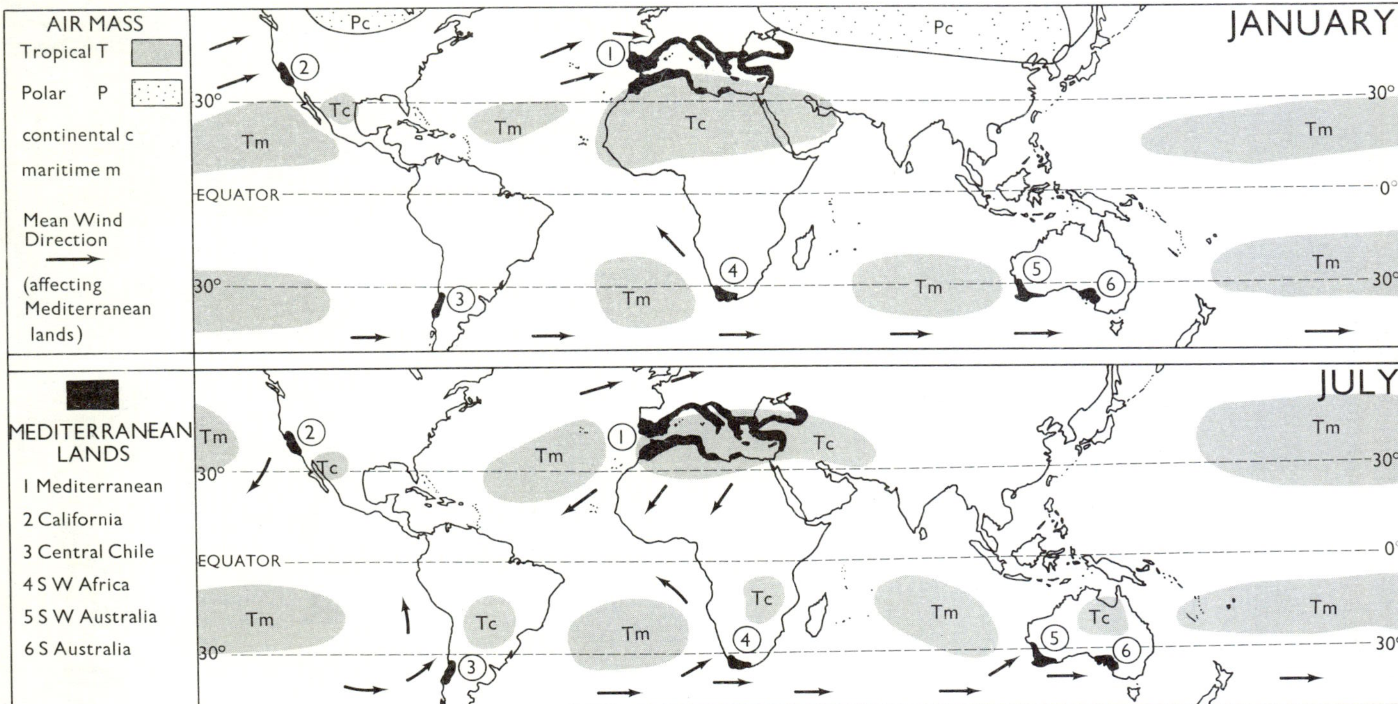

Fig. 4 A generalised view of the mean mid-summer and mid-winter location of those air masses which affect these Mediterranean lands (1–6). The influences of the prevailing westerlies is indicated and the absence of strong prevailing winds during the summer, when pressures are high. But such a simplified map masks climatic variability and ignores other climatic influences which are considered in the following pages.

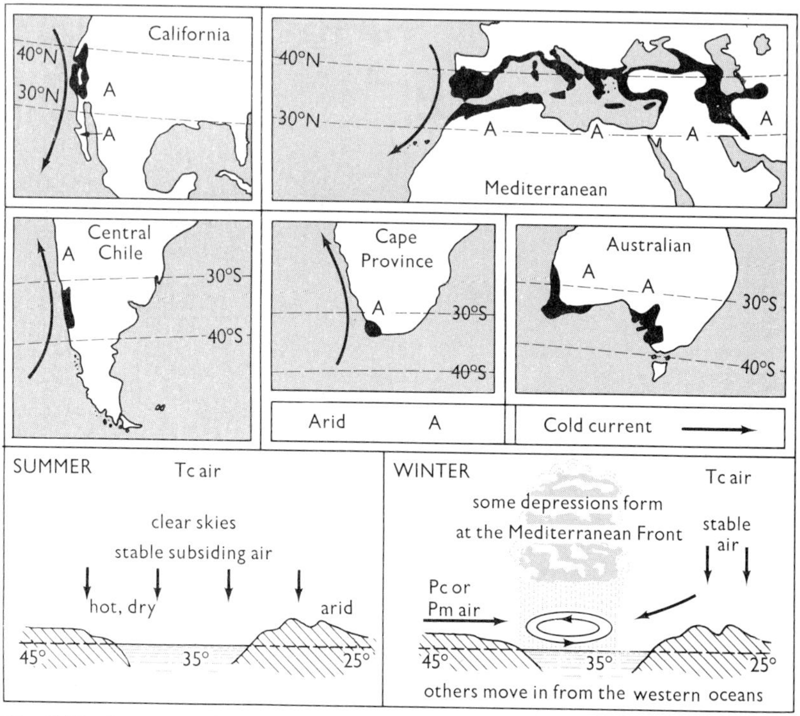

Fig. 5 The location of the Mediterranean lands and the off-shore cool currents. Sections show how conflicting air masses make for greater variability in winter than in summer in the countries about the Mediterranean Sea.

These broad annual climatic conditions are unique to what are generally known as the 'Mediterranean lands'—summers with long periods of clear skies and great heat; winters with changeable weather, but generally fairly mild. There are innumerable variations between and within these regions, and on p. 17 we look at particular climatic influences of soil–vegetation systems and at the other variables which affect those systems.

Effects on the Composition of the Vegetation

Areas affected by 'Mediterranean' conditions occur in different continents, and all display similar kinds of plant adaptations, though each has its own particular floristic composition. On a geological time-scale, this present, unique climate has affected them only relatively recently. World-wide climatic changes have taken place, and it is likely that summer rains gave way to summer drought only shortly before the Pleistocene, some two million years ago. Those plant species which at that time were growing in the drier habitats were best suited to survive and, by natural selection, to become dominant in the vegetation: these

Fig. 6 This protected security area, on limestone hills overlooking the re-settled, irrigated Metapontum Plain in southern Italy (Magna Graeca—p. 33), is closely wooded with evergreen oaks. Inland, the hills are grazed by goats and there is only maquis and garrigue.

included plants which had already developed small, leathery (sclerophyllous) leaves, and those which could more effectively draw up soil solutions during drought. Drying conditions favoured colonisation by species from adjacent dry zones—an invasion of the kind we see today where man's activities have led to desertification[1].

Ice advances during the Pleistocene did not destroy the existing vegetation, as they did in higher latitudes, although there were local modifications, especially in mountainous areas; so that each region contains plant communities with representatives of long-surviving families as well as species which have developed to suit their own particular habitats, and immigrants from adjacent zones.

Thus the composition of the present vegetation in each of the main floristic regions reflects (a) survivals from former climatic conditions, (b) adaptations to the present climate, (c) response to local relief and soil factors, (d) interference by man on a scale which has changed woodland to open shrub and herb communities.

In lands about the Mediterranean species of evergreen oak (*Quercus* sp.) were dominant in most of the original forests and are still common on the lowlands. The Holm oak and Kermes oak are widespread, but some species have regional dominance: the Cork oak (*Q. suber*), for example, is found mainly on siliceous soils in the western Mediterranean. Similarly, pines are common throughout, but Maritime pines are mostly on siliceous soils below 500 m and Umbrella pines up to 1000 m; while Aleppo pines grow mainly in the eastern Mediterranean.

The original forests sheltered a shrub layer, including such plants as

Fig. 7 A limestone surface in southern Crete, with young Grecian fir, low cushiony shrubs, asphodel's lily leaves, and broom.

box, viburnum, lentisc, and rose species, with a herb layer beneath. Some forest survives; but generally the Mediterranean landscapes are most typically made up of shrubby vegetation, cultivated trees, often of great antiquity, and local concentrations of intensive farming.

The taller shrub associations are generally known as *maquis* (Fr.), and, besides the plants mentioned above, include cistus, arbutus, heather, gorse and broom. The term 'maquis' embraces many different associations, usually named after the dominant species in a particular habitat: cistus maquis, for instance, covers much of the drier, hotter parts of the Mediterranean lands. Trees which have survived from earlier vegetation, like the Judas Tree, often stand among the maquis, together with trees such as the carob and olive which have been cultivated since ancient times.

Even more open vegetation, with lower, rounded shrubs, is commonly found in dry locations, especially on limestones and other pervious rocks, and may be a degraded form of maquis: it is known as *garrigue*. Many of the shrubs and herbs found in the maquis may be present, with such plants as thyme, sage, lavender and rosemary, which contain resinous aromatic oils and usually have tiny, leathery, hair-covered leaves. This 'rock heath' vegetation is usually a blaze of colour in spring, for there are also tuberous geophytes, such as tulips, crocuses, irises, garlic and *Orchis* species. Even the shrubs are absent in very dry areas of degraded vegetation. There are grasses, clovers, deep-rooted

Fig. 8 A hard, jointed limestone in eastern Crete, bearing garrigue vegetation and showing the effects of solution.

herbaceous perennials, and thistle-like plants of the daisy family. Some have underground storage organs, like the asphodel which is regarded as an indicator of impoverished soils.

Most of the maquis is the result of man's interference, but in dry locations—sheltered country among woodland, for example—it may be a climax vegetation, due to natural causes. The contrasts in altitude, degree of maritime influence, shelter, and soil characteristics give rise to many variations within these broad types of vegetation. About the Mediterranean, and on its many islands, earth movements and sea-level changes have isolated species of flora, which have developed along different lines from their relatives elsewhere.

Many plants have been introduced over the millennia, and have since spread. From the East came olives, figs and pomegranates and, much later, citrus fruits. Some recent introductions have quickly become widespread, like the Australian eucalypts and various succulents, such as the American prickly pear.

In California there is a general decrease in precipitation and increase in air temperature from north to south, and also climatic contrasts between the dry central valley and the western mountains, all of which are reflected in the vegetation. In the north, the woodland includes evergreen oaks and some deciduous species; but further south there is only patchy woodland among a sclerophyllous shrub formation with heathy plants,

Fig. 9 South African Cape plants: (*Left*) protea shrub, whose leaves have little tissue but a thick cuticle which prevents wilting; (*Right*) heathy plants with bright 'everlastings' on a sandy soil.

Fig. 10 A variety of flowering evergreen shrubs and spindly mallee eucalypts, north of the Stirling Range, south-west Australia: a type of maquis.

known as *chaparral*. Southwards the chaparral decreases in height and occurs at increasing altitude on hillsides. Many plant genera survived the Pleistocene climatic changes, including species of the shrub *Ceanothus*, which did not occur in Europe, though it has since been introduced, and the drought-resistant Piñon pine species.

There has been wholesale destruction of so much of California's plant-life, but the chaparral is a natural zonal vegetation in this Mediterranean region. Its composition responds to the low precipitation, winter rain and summer drought, and also to natural and man-made fires. After fire, many of its shrubs throw up new shoots (p. 31), and denser growth is encouraged: chaparral thus tends to expand at the expense of grassland and forest.

In Central Chile a dense sclerophyllous shrub formation, with taller trees, once covered much of central Chile. It was bounded in the north by the xerophytic vegetation of the arid zone; inland, above about 1400 m, by Andean alpine plants; and in the south, where there are only short dry spells during summer, by evergreen beeches and conifers.

Evergreen oaks are absent, but some tree and shrub species are remnants of former woodlands and peculiar to Chile, like the *Quillaja saponaria* of the rose family. On the whole, however, the Chilean *matorral* resembles the maquis and chaparral of the other regions.

In Cape Province, South Africa there are large areas of climatic climax sclerophyllous scrub, but also many places where the scrub vegetation is degraded from woodland. Many of the low bushy plants have small, leathery, blue-green leaves and, like the abundant Proteaceae, a number of them belong to families not found in the European Mediterranean. Various species of *Protea* occur as dominants in a low scrub, similar to dry maquis; most of them are deep-rooted and have large leaves with a thick cuticle, and can thrive on poor acidic soils. Here, too, fire tends to stimulate growth; and in the following year there is usually an abundance of herbs and geophytes, such as gladioli, for the shrubs, developing from seeds or shoots, take a few years to re-establish themselves.

In South-West Australia plant life-forms are very similar to those in other sclerophyllous formations. In the drier parts, many of the shrubby plants belong to the genus *Eucalyptus*, often in mallee form with branches springing from an underground tuberous stem. There are also shrubs of other genera not naturally represented in European flora, and many of the brightly flowering geophytes are unique to south-west Australia. The Proteaceae also occur here and are often dominant in sandy areas: the unusual *Xanthorrhoea* ('grass tree') of the lily family is found, with mallee heath, on sandy soils. Here again the variety of soils, from those on the coastal limestones and sands to those developed on the granites and iron-rich duricrusts of the low interior tableland, makes for many variations in plant associations.

The composition of the vegetation with its dominant *Eucalyptus* species also changes with the rainfall, which decreases northwards and inland of Perth. In the wetter south-west there are forests of the tall eucalypts jarrah and karri, with trees up to 85 m in height.

Enormous areas of the scrubland have been cleared for wheat and sheep farming on soils boosted by superphosphate addition, but they readily revert to mallee when neglected or abandoned.

In South Australia the winter rain areas of the south-east corner of South Australia and north-east Victoria also bear dry sclerophyllous vegetation with mallee scrub, stretches of eucalypt woodland, heaths with proteas, and occasional 'grass trees'. Here, as in the other Mediterranean lands, habitats favouring plant development are now occupied by vineyards or other crops, and the 'wildscape' vegetation tends to grow under less favourable conditions.

Fig. 11 (*Left*) sclerophyllous *Banksia attentuata* with narrow leaves and woody stem. (*Right*) Tall, straight karri eucalypts, in south-west Australia.

External Variables
I Climatic Influences

Sub-types of Mediterranean Climate

The climatic regimes of the Mediterranean regions shown in Fig. 4 are often summarised as 'warm, wet winters; hot, dry summers'. But each has recognisable climatic sub-divisions, quite apart from micro-climatic

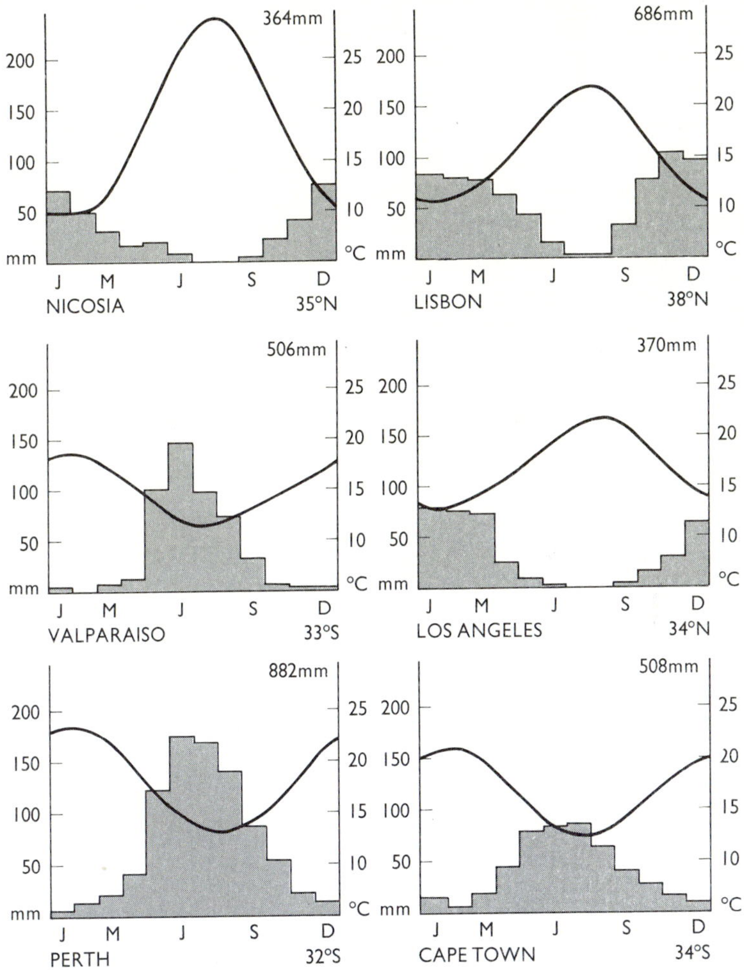

Fig. 12 Mean monthly precipitation and temperature. Los Angeles and Nicosia represent noticeably drier sub-types of climate, though their temperate ranges reflect maritime and continental influences respectively.

variations due to local relief, soils, aspect and so on[2]. Some reflect maritime influences in their more moderate temperatures and higher rainfall, others show the effects of a more continental location. This is true of lands in and about the Mediterranean Sea, where climates are also affected by the inclusion of this large volume of water by the Euro-Asian and African continents, and by the great contrasts in structure and relief; there are also latitudinal differences in climatic regimes: thus in the the north spring and autumn rainfall maxima are usual. Much of south-west Australia is affected climatically by the huge dry landmass to the north and east; but in the south there are also strong maritime influences. The climate of central Chile is modified by the cold waters of the Peru (Humboldt) Current. Here are variations due to altitude differences, and to the alignment of the coastal mountains, central valley and Andean barrier, which produces rainshadow effects.

The mean data used in Fig. 12 show some of the regional variations, but mask the variability of these climates, especially in the drier locations; and, of course, *actual* temperature and rainfall figures would reveal much greater differences from place to place, and from time to time. Despite all the differences, however, there are common patterns in the climatic regimes of these broad regions. We will now consider how they affect the various plant–soil systems.

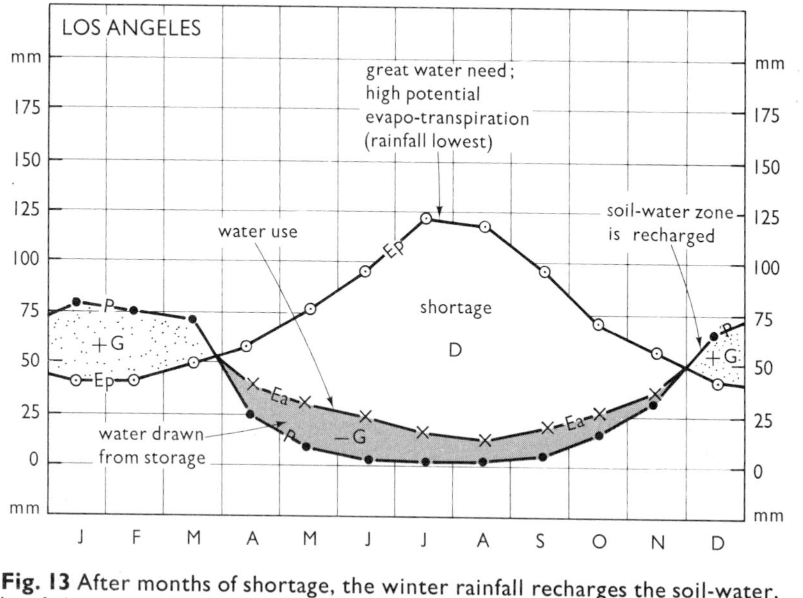

Fig. 13 After months of shortage, the winter rainfall recharges the soil-water, but fails to create a surplus. Ep—Ea shows the extra water needed to maintain a plant–leaf soil coverage.

Soil-water Fluctuations and Plant Responses

The lack of precipitation during the hottest parts of the year, when the loss of water through evapo-transpiration should be great, suggests that the soil-water balance within the chosen system may be critical. Figs. 13 and 14 show how this fluctuates through the year at Los Angeles and at Perth, Western Australia, using data from Thornthwaite/Strahler[3] for:

P	precipitation	[mean figures are used (mm)]
Ea	actual evapo-transpiration (water returned to the atmosphere from plants and ground surface)	actual water *used* in passage from soil storage to atmosphere
Ep	potential evapo-transpiration (estimated loss from a surface covered by the leaves of plants always supplied with adequate water)	water *needed* to maintain the complete plant/leaf cover
D	soil-water shortage (Ep—Ea)	could be made up by irrigation
G	represents a change in the soil-water storage	–G indicates withdrawal +G indicates recharge
R	surplus water	may be lost by overland flow or by percolation to groundwater

Los Angeles lies in a dry sub-type of Mediterranean climate. There the winter rains recharge the soil-water resources after the summer drought, but do not create a water surplus. Storage withdrawal begins in April, but the plants later reduce their water use. The difference between Ep and Ea indicates that large quantities of water are needed to maintain a plant cover.

In such dry climates the plants adapt in different ways to reduce moisture loss. The leaves of the evergreen trees and shrubs have thick outer cell layers, and their stomata, or leaf pores, are closed by guard cells during the hotter parts of the day. In some heath species the leaf hairs close over the stomata. Reduction in leaf size, and thus in the area of transpiration, is seen in many garrigue plants. The oil content of fragrant shrubs also helps to reduce transpiration. Many of the sclerophylls are able to absorb more soil-water as the increase in the concentration of their cell-sap causes a rise in osmotic pressure; for though high cell-sap concentration dehydrates the protoplasm, their thick-celled leaves stand up to this without wilting[1]. Other plants, however, like *Cistus*, shed their leaves as the cell-sap concentration increases. Such plants are not deep-rooted. Succulents, with water-storing tissues, such as the aloes and cacti-like species of *Euphorbia*, are also found in the drier parts.

There are responses to conditions like those shown in Fig. 13; but this does not indicate the most intensive periods of growth or flowering. Perennial trees and shrubs not only decline in activity during drought, but also when the temperature is low; which is a factor even in dry regions, and an important one in the northern Mediterranean, for example. Autumn growth follows the summer drought, and many geophytes flower at this time. During spring, when solar radiation increases and soil moisture is available, there is an intensive period of growth and flowering. But by mid-summer the vegetation has a drab appearance, for few plants are in flower, many have lost their leaves, and herbs have withered.

The soil-water budget for Perth shows similar fluctuations, but being in a more humid climatic sub-region, there is a period of water surplus. During October, after the winter rains, there is withdrawal from soil-water storage; but after the initial surge in growth and water removal, there is a fall in demand as plants reduce their water requirements. There is then a shortage for six months before rainfall rapidly recharges the soil-water storage; by July there is a water surplus.

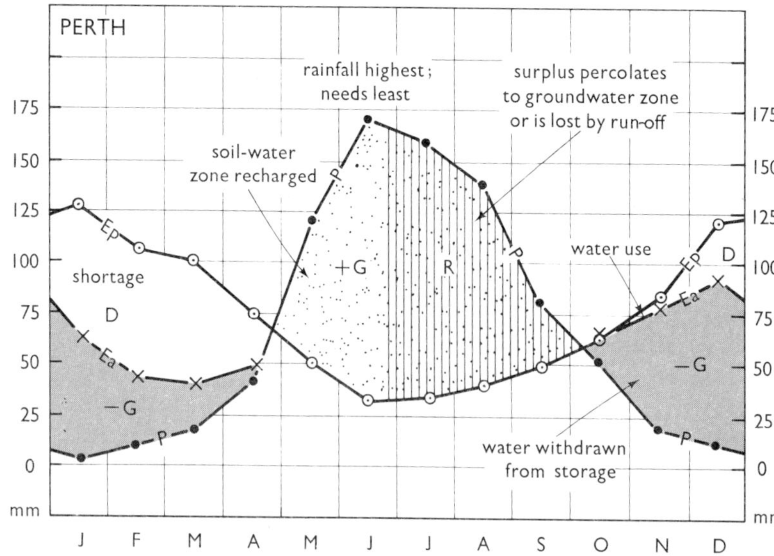

Fig. 14 Here, after a seven-month shortage, winter rainfall recharges the soil-water zone and creates a surplus for a three-month period.

In this part of the sub-region there is evergreen woodland, though much has been cleared for agricultural and urban land-use. Further south, the eucalypt forests still flourish. But the mean figures do not give a complete picture, for the annual rainfall is very variable, and for years at a time soil-water storage may be far short of that suggested by Fig. 14.

Many of the hundreds of *Eucalyptus* species found in Australia have been successfully introduced into other Mediterranean lands. Their sclerophyllous habit, together with their leaf oils and twisting leaf stalks which keep them edgeways to the sun, helps to prevent water loss. Their responses to fire are described on p. 31.

Inland, where the drier type of climate prevails, there is often bare earth between the mallee eucalypts, acacias and other leguminous shrubs. These, like the proteas, grow mainly on sandy soils. Here there is no regular, seasonal water surplus.

Climate and the Soils

We have seen that evergreen forests maintain a relatively moist soil environment and add humus to the deepish, pale-brown soils, usually called 'brown earths'. Fig. 15 shows that beneath the humus-rich A zone light leaching removes clay minerals; this leaves a lighter horizon above the darker, clayey, illuviated one, where precipitated iron compounds give a reddish colour. Where the parent rock is limestone, fissures in the lower horizons may be filled with red clay.

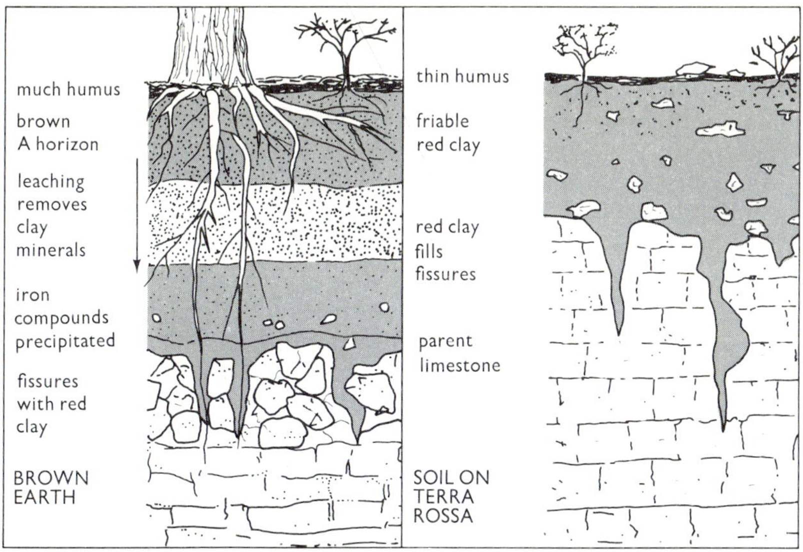

Fig. 15 (*Left*) Horizons in a brown earth formed beneath a tree-shrub cover. (*Right*) Red, clayey 'terra rossa' soil over weathered limestone.

Fig. 16 Garrigue on red clay, which fills a fissure in jointed, weathered limestone in eastern Crete.

However, even when such forests were widespread, there was in fact a variety of soils in the lands about the Mediterranean Sea. High rainfall, especially in the mountains of the western Mediterranean, caused much leaching and produced podsolised soils. In other places, large areas of hard, jointed limestones acquired karst characteristics. Chemical actions, especially during the warmer, humid periods, encouraged the gradual solution and disappearance of great thicknesses of carbonate. Many of the impurities they contained remained unaltered, and accumulated in varying thicknesses, forming soils whose basicity favoured the retention of red iron oxides during moist periods. Where the vegetation provided sufficient humus these soils appeared reddish-brown. Elsewhere, soils were formed on materials of volcanic origin and supported vegetation which responded to their basicity or acidity, and to their water-holding properties. Heaths on volcanic ash contrasted with woodland on basic lavas.

Such variations remain. But the climatic and soil-water fluctuations described above now affect habitats changed by deforestation, grazing or cultivation. For thousands of years the winter rains have fallen on exposed surfaces parched by summer drought, and run-off has eroded friable soils and poorly consolidated sedimentaries, sweeping loosened material downslope. The autumn rains, in particular, are often heavy, though of short duration, and cause much erosion. The shrub vegetation

Fig. 17 Olives on thin soils on a hillside in southern Spain; in places erosion has stripped the limestone bare. Each tree is rooted in soil in a prepared trench.

which now covers so much of these landscapes provides less humus and, with so little shade, even this rapidly breaks down and can no longer bind soil particles. Exposure also leads to a lowering of the water-table, so that there is a higher proportion of xerophytic plants, and vegetation degradation allows the materials to move downslope even more readily. Even the gentler surfaces tend to become gravelly as the finer particles are removed.

Massive talus slopes are common in these regions (p. 41). These have a mixture of minerals, which may form solutions in water draining from above, so that they are sometimes able to support shrub vegetation and re-establish a soil; though the downslope movements make it difficult for any clear horizons to develop. The water acquires solutions of the more soluble salts, so that the pH value of the talus soils may be different from those on the parent rock, and thus favour different plants. For instance, soils on talus material which have a higher pH value than those on parent siliceous sandstones may favour rosemary garrigue rather than the heathy maquis on the rocks above.

The clearance of woodland from the reddish earths covering hard karstic limestones has caused much degradation and loss of soil material, so that we now find gravelly soils supporting, for example, small, scattered Kermes oaks, rooted in cracks, or perhaps dwarf palms and almost bare limestones with spiky asphodels. But where the impurities left by solution have accumulated in depressions, and are no longer stained by abundant humus, they form a rich red 'terra rossa', with much more fertile soils than those on the neighbouring limestones and, where water is available, may build up a humus content. They often support an interculture of grain and tree crops. The soils are usually of dark red clay. The upper part with some organic matter is friable, but the firmer clay beneath tends to become plastic when wet. Many of them are stony throughout, and extend deep into cracks and fissures in the weathered limestone.

Colour alone is not an adequate guide to the nature of Mediterranean soils. Red soils are widespread: some are relic terra rossa, some derived from brown earths; some are clays derived from red Triassic sandstones or from fine red particles brought by winds from arid lands; others are formed from iron-rich volcanic materials.

Former climatic conditions have influenced both the nature and the distribution of soils in other Mediterranean lands. In the drier interior of south-west Australia, for example, nutrient-poor sandy and gravelly soils cover iron-rich duricrusts, which are relics of an earlier pluvial period. The fluctuating water-table of those wetter times caused insoluble ferric compounds to form a hard layer beneath the surface. The breakdown of the now exposed crust provides sandy material, as does the weathering of the ancient granites of these low interior tablelands. But though today's climate may be only indirectly responsible for the composition and nutrient status of soils in these and other parts of the Mediterranean lands, the present regime controls the provision of soil-water and soluble nutrients to plants, and its own fluctuations create a high risk of soil erosion.

Climate and Human Activities

Men and their domestic animals have disturbed the Mediterranean plant–soil systems for a very long time, and their behaviour is considered on p. 31 as part of the external variables belonging to the biosphere. Climatic conditions have always had a great bearing on the way men behave, and there is space here only to summarise their broad influences on settlement in and about the Mediterranean Sea:

(a) In lands which do not experience the severities of arctic cold, or tropical conditions of great heat and high humidity, a rural life can be one of relative comfort, despite the annual combat with drought. Generally, the mild winters with sunny spells and the hot, dry sunny summers have allowed a wide variety of plants to be cultivated wherever they could be rooted in fertile soils with adequate moisture. The Greek city-states exploited the fertility of isolated valley sites, deltas and raised beaches; and even before this the Minoans in Crete and the Mycenaeans

Fig. 18 Difficult ploughing on stony lime-rich valley soil, near Arvi in southern Crete. Notice the loose scree on the valley sides. Comparison with Fig. 19 illustrates the particular importance of local environmental conditions to Mediterranean agriculture.

Fig. 19 Deep soils, on the naturally drained lake bed of the high Lasithi Plains, in central Crete, produce an oasis of intensive commercial farming, where traditional methods, like these, are combined with seed selection and soil treatment to maintain high fertility.

on the mainland had developed civilised life in a climate which suited the blend of hard work and leisure so typical of Mediterranean communities.

(b) The climate has allowed many plants from other climatic regions to be introduced successfully, and trade by sea encouraged their spread and exchange between Mediterranean lands. By the second millennium BC, the vine and cultivated olive had spread from Asia Minor into the eastern Mediterranean. The Romans first created great vineyards and brought citrus fruits from south-east Asia, and later the Moors established vineyards in the western Mediterranean. Arab traders helped to introduce mulberries, cherries and apricots from Asia Minor, and also tropical and sub-tropical crops such as bananas, varieties of cotton, sugar cane, rice and spices. Irrigation systems provided the soil moisture and greatly extended the area under cultivation.

(c) The Sea is fringed by much bold relief, and affected from autumn to spring by air circulations which, at times, draw cold air from the north or hot, dusty air from the south. Such local conditions have affected men through the ages. The changeability is reflected in the numerous shipwrecks of Greek legend and Biblical narrative. The bitterly cold, spring Mistral can still wither the blossoms of southern France. Variations in altitude, shelter and exposure create many local climatic regions within these lands.

(d) The effects of forest clearance, vegetation degradation and the exposure of skeletal soils in a climatic regime in which heavy rains follow lengthy desiccation have already been discussed. The hillsides are still being stripped for expanding settlement and haphazard development, and, unfortunately, frequent earth tremors are apt to trigger soil slips on slopes which have become unstable.

(e) The dry sunny summers and the maritime influences encourage tourism in the coastal areas. This may be beneficial to the local economy and promote desirable social changes, but can create many forms of pollution and cause less desirable social stresses—an ambivalence inherent in general mass tourism.

II The Influence of Local Rocks

In some parts of the world, climatic and geomorphic influences combine to produce physical features characteristic of particular parent rocks, such as the massive screes below frost-shattered shales in periglacial lands[4] and the domed inselbergs of jointed granitic rock in the humid tropics[5]. The betwixt-and-between climates and complex tectonic activities in the Mediterranean lands make it difficult to generalise about 'typical landforms'. Some of the physical features undoubtedly owe their present form to past climatic conditions—many solution features of the karst limestones in Jugoslavia relate to warmer, wetter, interglacial periods, and the mesas of central Cyprus (Fig. 36) to past fluvial activities as well as to weathering under present semi-arid conditions.

It is common to find many different types of rocks within quite small areas. Recent sands and clays often adjoin the widespread Mesozoic limestones. Elsewhere they abut plutonic masses, or are covered by more recent volcanic flows. Many of the countries display sequences of older rocks exposed by Alpine folding or over-folding. This frequently produced cultural as well as physical variety, for local rocks do have considerable influence on both physical conditions and the human environment.

Fig. 20 An upland of calanchi, with slips and slumps of Pliocene sands and clays, clearly seen beyond the faulted valley edge, at Ferrandina in south-central Italy. Natural gas and chemical works have recently revitalised this sparsely settled region.

Fig. 21 (*Left*) Solution has pitted this limestone surface in northern Malta, where plants grow in shallow soil pockets, and has enlarged pre-historic sled tracks, which continue beyond the fallen cliff-edge. (*Right*) Solution followed by precipitation has created stalactites, exposed by cave collapse in maquis-covered limestones in western Crete.

In many parts of the Mediterranean there are elevated sedimentaries consisting of loose porous sandstones or calcareous marls overlying a bed of clay. When rain soaks in and lubricates the sandstone/clay face it is apt to cause mass movement, especially on slopes. Such movement is particularly frequent in earthquake zones, such as central southern Italy, where a long succession of slips and slumps has created badlands (*calanchi*)[6]. On the other hand, level-bedded sands and clays also make up the coastal flats and terraces which have been farmed from ancient times; for with a relatively high water-table, and often impregnated by limy solutions, they are able to support cereal crops, fruit trees and vegetables.

Agricultural land-use varies a great deal with the type of rock. This is illustrated by the variety found on volcanic rocks in quite a small area. About the Alban hills, south of Rome, soils weathered from basalt support vineyards and fruit trees in a well-populated countryside; but a little to the north the thick, soft tuff deposits of volcanic ash, sometimes with hard crusts and usually deeply eroded, have poorly cultivated grainlands and neglected areas with maquis (*macchia*). Here and there, are slopes of volcanic ash which support only acid-tolerant shrubs.

Limestones of varying hardness and purity, and partly cemented calcareous sandstones occur in many parts of the Mediterranean. The formation of blocky pavements and caverns in the harder, jointed limestones is not entirely due to past conditions. There is much evidence

Fig. 22 Close cultivation of scree slopes, whose looseness is shown by the debris slide on the left, and by slips on these garrigue-covered hillsides in central Crete.

of continuing solution; and, despite dry summers, lichens and mosses often colonise the rocks and create organic acids which help rainwater dissolve out oval depressions in the surface. These rocks tend to support poor garrigue and herds of goats, in contrast to the tree crops and grain cultivation on terra rossa and other sedimentaries.

In these climates, solution often creates a hard capping on the softer limestones. Water soaks into the pervious rock and solutions drawn up during drought deposit calcium carbonate, which forms a crust near the surface. These hard layers may be seen overhanging the edge of a retreating rock face, and often provide animal shelters. The sparse plant coverage exposes many of the less consolidated rocks, but there is not necessarily gullying, for water readily sinks in. Besides the surface features caused by solution, gradual chemical changes are also revealed by the spheroidal weathering of boulders within rock masses.

Particular rocks may weather to different degrees in the different climatic sub-regions. Granites in the wetter, highland parts of Corsica experienced chemical weathering and hydration during Quaternary interglacials, often to depths of 30 m or so. Granular disintegration produced a mantle of rotted rock. Where forest has been removed, the present climate leads to deep gullying over the ancient crystallines. By contrast, the granite exposures in South Africa's Mediterranean south-west remain massive, with only thin acidic soils which, like the overlying Table Mountain sandstones, support erica and protea shrubs.

The influence of rocks extends to the exploitation of their mineral

Fig. 23 Cape Town, where hard, jointed Table Mountain sandstone overlies the massive, rounded granite exposed at the sea edge. Immense talus slopes have built up, and slips are common along the Hout Bay road, seen on the far headland.

content, which does not necessarily relate to present climatic conditions. Mining ranges from Cyprus' copper and asbestos to south-west Australia's coal and ilmenite. Strangely, gold has stimulated settlement in three of the Mediterranean regions: following the Californian finds of 1848; after the rush to Kalgoorlie in the early 1890s, though wheat, wool and timber production was already well established in south-west Australia; and indirectly boosted by the Witwatersrand finds of 1886, which gave economic strength for the development of the far distant, established Cape Colony and its main port. The development of warm temperate Chile has also owed more to the desert's nitrates and copper than to the agricultural assets of the region itself, despite its long history of settlement.

The release of elements from the rocks by weathering has particular regional significance for the various plant–soil systems. Parent rock may play a dominant role where the soils are so often skeletal or immature. Its influence is not simply due to a supply of potential nutrients; it may also act restrictively. Many limestones and calcareous sandstones, for instance, give soils a high pH value, which causes iron to be retained chemically and not be available for absorption. Thus shrubs like camellias which require a high iron intake would be excluded, even though conditions were sufficiently warm and moist.

III The Biosphere: Human Dominance

It is already apparent that most of the climatic climax vegetation of the Mediterranean lands, with stable plant associations adapted to the seasonal moisture fluctuations, has suffered from human interference including deliberate and accidental firing. However, fires also occur through natural causes, such as lightning, and their effects are not simply destructive.

Fire and Its Effects

The fires which sweep through maquis, chaparral and eucalypt scrubland make headlines when they threaten rural settlement or expanding suburban populations: but their effects on the vegetation are often, in part, beneficial. In the chaparral, few sprouting shrubs are killed. New shoots from survivors eventually form thick bushes, which gradually shade out the abundant herbaceous growth which occurs after fire. After some five years, the shrubby vegetation may be denser than before. The Australian bush fires are often very fierce, due both to dry litter, from bark as well as leaves, and the vaporisation of the leaf oils of the sclerophylls. Fires spread rapidly. But after fire many eucalypts sprout from buds beneath the bark, and nutrients released from litter derived from Proteaceae, like *Banksia sp.*, and from 'grass trees', stimulate new growth. In fact, grass trees bloom only after fire, and *Banksia* is a pyrophyte which does not regenerate until fire causes its woody fruits to open. Many of the seeds, like those of chaparral species, are resistant to heat injury, and some are stimulated to develop by the heat.

Unduly fierce heat may do much damage: whereas frequent light firing removes litter and may help to prevent a fierce, prolonged blaze. Much depends on the plant species present. In the chaparral, non-sprouting species of *Ceanothus* and other plants may be killed by rapidly recurring fires, as well as by intense heat. Vegetation regeneration is also affected by the tendency for soil erosion to increase during the first year after fire, with a loss of plant nutrients. Ecological adjustments are often complex. In California, the grasses and broad-leaved herbs which rapidly colonise burnt chaparral provide extra grazing for deer, so that their reproductive rate rises for a short period after fire; but a larger deer population can lead to soil erosion.

Fire is also ecologically important for South Africa's Cape flora. We have seen that many of the soils are acidic and poor in nutrients, which

Fig. 24 A group of *Xanthorroea*, 'grass trees', blooming after fire which has blackened their stems and the trunks of the eucalypts. A dense ground stratum of various herbs is well established.

suits proteas and heathy plants; but after fire numerous geophytes, herbaceous species, and dwarf shrubs come into their own, for root competition is removed and the ashes provide nutrients. They usually compete successfully for some four or five years.

Man's Use and Modification of the Soil–Vegetation Systems

Many agrarian systems have been established during the long history of settlement about the Mediterranean: simple pastoralism and subsistence farming by family groups; patterns of cultivation organised by the ancient Greeks to support colonisation; land ownership consolidated by the Romans; and so on through the ages to current land reforms like those in southern Italy. Old methods survived, overlapping the new, as they do today. All have left imprints on the largely man-made Mediterranean landscapes. A few instances must serve to show how men modified the vegetation–soil systems of their place and time.

Early Development of Land Management

The ancient Greek city-states soon experienced repercussions caused by their successful settlement on limited cultivable land. While carefully selected lowland soils supported the growing community, woodland was progressively stripped from the hills for charcoal and timber, and shrub vegetation, fired to extend pastoralism, was further degraded by sheep and goats. Even as the growing population put pressure on the land, soil erosion fretted the denuded slopes. Wise men advocated planned land-use. In Attica, in 313 BC, Theophrastus urged men to 'use your rich soils for grain and your thin soils for trees. Grain and all other annuals take the nutriment from the surface soil which, therefore, ought not to be thin or of a quality to be quickly exhausted, as happens in a shallow layer of earth. But trees equipped with long and strong roots, draw nourishment from depth'.[7] These were practical people, who built deep wells and diverted springs and, as in their Magna Graeca colonies in southern Italy, both irrigated the level raised beaches and reclaimed adjoining coastal marshland.

The Roman influence was widespread. The demands of a civilisation with hundreds of colonial towns accelerated deforestation; but new technologies and engineering skills enabled them to divert lakes through tunnels, drain marshes by canals, and build aqueducts for distant irrigation. Land-use was regulated. As grain tributes poured in from their Empire, they varied the long-established pattern of olives on thin hill soils, vines on lower slopes and cereals on lowland, so that tree crops and extensive vineyards covered the richer lands. In many places families were settled on rectangular holdings within large *centuria quadrata*, whose roads and drainage channels formed a reticulated pattern still to be seen in parts of Italy.

But then, as now, soil conditions largely controlled land-use: irrigable soils were mostly alluvial in origin; dry farming was best suited by neutral, or slightly alkaline soils and thin soils with little moisture supported rough grazing. Later, other people, notably the Moors, who pioneered many of the irrigation systems in North Africa and Spain, extended the area of arable land especially by skilful terracing.

The Changing Patterns of Land-use

With so much rugged relief, settlement has always been scattered, with intervening wildscape, modified by pastoralism. The destruction of the climatic climax forms of vegetation continued over the ages; but continuity of cultivation has often been interrupted by events which disturbed settled societies and created new settlement patterns. For example, much of the long-settled, well drained coastal lands in southern Italy reverted to malarial swamp when Roman control ended. As crusading armies and other marauders moved along the flanks of the Italian peninsula, vulnerable fertile lowlands were abandoned for greater security in hill settlements. Until recent reclamation, through drainage and anti-malarial spraying, re-established intensive farming along the coast, most of southern Italy's rural population lived in hill towns, amid limestones with thin soils and loose sedimentaries which readily created badlands (p. 28).

Fig. 25 Cave settlements in hard Cretaceous limestones, about the hill town of Matera in southern Italy. These furnished caves housed nearly 20 000 people before re-settlement in the 1950s.

This is a particularly telling example of the vicious circle of land mismanagement so often found in the Mediterranean lands:

MISMANAGEMENT OF HILLY LAND → SOIL EROSION → SILTING OF ESTUARIES → MALARIA → MORE PEOPLE RETREAT TO HILLS → MORE SOIL EROSION

Even though malaria is mostly eradicated, silted harbours and poor drainage are still features of many Mediterranean coastlands.

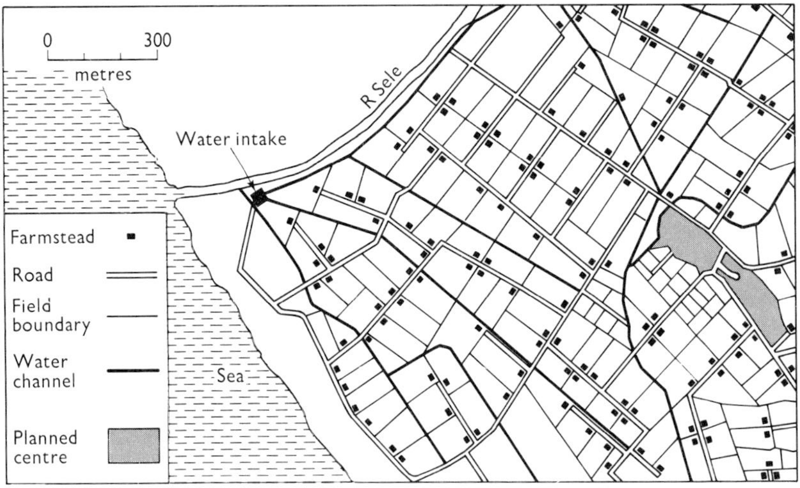

Fig. 26 An example of re-settlement of Italian hill families on the Sele Plain. The planned centre, Gromola, serves farmers growing vegetables and fruits by intensive, irrigated cultivation. New factories prepare and pack tomatoes and other produce.

Fig. 27 Land adjoining the village of Zania in central Crete has small labour-intensive holdings. Beyond are olives, with grain growing beneath the trees, and above are hillsides where sheep are tended.

From Iberia to the Middle East, people have responded to similar climatic and edaphic (soil) constraints in similar ways. In the mountains of Crete, as in the Atlas, are small isolated settlements where peasant families have based their lives mainly on pastoralism. Elsewhere transhumance was, until recently, a traditional response to the climatic regime—in Italy, Iberia, and North Africa alike. Millions of sheep were moved annually from the Spanish Meseta to summer mountain pastures, and back in the autumn. But most typical of the Mediterranean countries are the many nucleated settlements, from which, over the ages, families have daily set out by foot, or animal transport, to work the fields. Land-use was adjusted according to distance and activity. In many cases, it is still possible to recognise the inner zone of intensive cultivation of vegetables and fruits, the arable land beyond with cereals and tree crops, and olives and vineyards further out, until increasing amounts of fallow land give way to rough pasture.

But today, with road improvements and the introduction of motor cycles, small-engined tractors, plastic hosing, and fertilisers, the pattern tends to break down, especially where soils can be improved and demands for rural produce increase. The transformation is often surprisingly rapid. The landscape of southern Crete has been transformed in a few years from traditional cultivation about hill settlements and small fishing villages to a scene of intensive, mechanised cultivation of vegetables, especially tomatoes. An improved road connects the country either side of Ierapetra to the northern ports. At first the coastal flats became a mini-township of long greenhouses, roofed with semi-transparent fabric. Then the loose sedimentaries of the

Fig. 28 Plastic sheeting covers greenhouses crowded on to terraces newly cut into the hillsides near Ierapetra, southern Crete: notice the truck and stacks of tomato boxes (right).

Fig. 29 Closely cultivated, terraced hillsides near Skopi, Crete, where water pumped from below represents a different form of energy input from that of the animals which once trod the circular threshing floor (left).

steep hillsides were terraced to hold more and more of them. New warehouses, garages for excavators and trucks, and stacks of packing boxes line the narrow coast road, and fuel-powered engines augment water supplies from hundreds of traditional windpumps. Visual pollution is as evident as the serious erosion of the hastily cleared slopes, surely predictable in this type of climate.

Developments of this kind reflect man's demands, technological improvements and organising abilities, but are still responses to the local conditions—to the mild frost-free spring with long periods of unbroken sunshine, to suitable aspect, soil factors, and sub-artesian water.

Energy Inputs and Production

This particular Cretan example of transformation really reflects an increased energy input[8]: energy to make, supply and power machines for road building, transport, excavation and water pumping; energy used in making and delivering fertilisers, pesticides and the processed sheeting which maximises solar energy through the greenhouse effect.

The main patterns of settlement in other Mediterranean regions have been established since the energy/industrial revolution. California has been developed in an industrial-technological age with huge inputs of energy. Here, where much of the central valley is semi-arid (though with a rainfall regime similar to that of the moister, adjacent 'Mediterranean' parts), productivity has depended on the control of the waters of the Sacramento and San Joaquin rivers, and on energy and irrigation water from more distant systems. It has been boosted by the development of increasingly efficient mechanical transport, farm machinery, and means of processing and packing fruits and vegetables grown under scientific control. Here the wine industry is on a large scale, and mechanised. But again, the natural assets are important—the climatic attributes, the fertile light soils of the central valley and deltaic alluvium. Nevertheless, the large output depends on energy from dams and fossil fuels as well as on solar energy, and this passes through the whole system from plant growth to processing, in a factory-like sequence. Climate stimulates migration to this, the most populous State, known for its films and tourism, which indirectly leads to industrial development.

In South Africa a large amount of energy in the form of fertilisers is put into the shallow, stony soils north of Cape Town to support large-scale wheat growing. Vines were established three hundred years ago. Now scientific research, cooperative association, and a large energy input enables thousands of growers to produce varieties to suit local micro-climates, soils and topography. Irrigation is widely used. The well drained, fertile sandy loams, weathered from granite, support most vines on gentle eastward-facing slopes; cooler, higher slopes are best for dry

Fig. 30 A pattern of intensive fruit farms and vineyards in South Africa's Cape Province, with reservoirs, fenced fields, service roads and factories representing a large energy input.

wines, the lower valleys for heavier, sweeter ones. Natural advantages are used and carefully modified.

Western Australia's dry climatic sub-region is also a major wheat producer; but the climatic advantages are tempered by prolonged droughts and hail, which can seriously affect the individual farmer. Here, too, great inputs of energy are needed, for wheat is grown on huge properties by a small labour force, using much machinery and large applications of superphosphate. The relatively low yield per hectare is typical of extensive farming; but a network of railways carries a huge volume of grain to the ports. There is intensive cultivation of fruit and vegetables on small farms in the forested south-west.

Mediterranean Chile has long suffered from a land ownership system of huge pastoral estates with under-utilisation of arable land, and peasant holdings too small to support a family. Yet the central valley has potential similar to fertile parts of other Mediterranean lands. The great estates irrigate pastures, grow alfalfa and wheat, and maintain vineyards, yet lack the organisation and energy input which characterise developments in California, South Africa and Australia. Today's small holdings have increased production of deciduous and citrus fruits and vegetables; yet land distribution problems remain—an apt example of man as a 'variable' affecting plant-soil relationships.

IV The Effects of Morphogenic Processes

We have already seen how the typical seasonal variations in rainfall and soil moisture affect mass movement of surface material, soil minerals and vegetation. But, again, generalisations about 'geomorphic features typical of the Mediterranean lands' are likely to be of little value; for there is such a variety of small regions, and the peripheral parts of the Mediterranean land areas exhibit similarities to their neighbouring zones—European temperate to the north and west, semi-arid to the south and east. Yet certain geomorphic processes can be particularly active, as shown by the drastic results induced by man, and this gives a uniqueness to the Mediterranean zone.

That the present climatic regime is significant is shown by the characteristics of the rivers, which do not receive run-off for months on end, at a time when groundwater contributions are also low, so that many of them lack a main perennial water channel. However, the sparse plant cover allows much winter storm run-off, direct to rivers, and can produce torrents capable of moving large boulders. As the floods subside gravelly mounds are deposited, which cause braiding. Debris-strewn torrent beds, with steep, undercut banks, are characteristic of the Mediterranean lands; many of them are dry during summer. The generally low seasonal rainfall also favours the accumulation of large amounts of scree below weathering rock faces.

Fig. 31 The river bed at Peristerona, Cyprus, shows the large load moved and deposited during winter storms, and the small spring flow, which will dry completely during the summer.

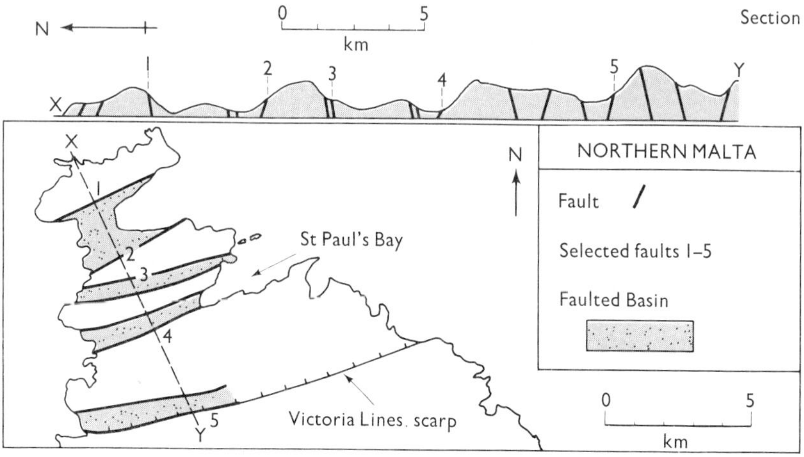

Fig. 32 The main geomorphological features of northern Malta are fault-guided blocks and basins, with almost parallel escarpments.

Thus it is possible to recognise elements of the landscape which are common to these lands; but yet it is difficult to point to morphological features which are *uniquely* 'Mediterranean'. Here the landforms, as well as the plant–soil characteristics, owe much to causes which vary in space and time: (a) tectonics related to plate movements; (b) associated volcanic activity; (c) glacial and post-glacial sea-level changes;

Fig. 33 Earth movements have created a major slip, with a sheer ten-metre face, running across the mountains of eastern Crete, as seen here above the village of Lastros. Fig. 34 shows fault-bounded blocks in the same area.

(d) climatic features in the past; (e) present climatic and hydrological conditions; (f) human interference.

The lands about the Mediterranean have been greatly disturbed by Alpine mountain building, and by the numerous deep-seated fractures and vertical displacements associated with plate movements in this collision zone. Hence we find landscapes like those in Malta, where parallel ridges and valleys are related to horsts and rifts. Fig. 32 shows that northern Malta is dominated by faults striking NNE, and is bounded in the south by the cliff-like face of a fault-scarp[9]. The following examples also show tectonic activity as a major morphological influence, and illustrate the effects of climatic conditions, past and present.

In Cyprus, most rural settlement north of the Kyrenia Range is on a piedmont dissected by deep transverse valleys[10]. The villages, with fields and rough, shrubby grazing land about them, are high above these valleys, on flat terraces standing at different levels. About a million years ago, the sea was some 250 m above its present level, and the climate much wetter. Strong rivers brought down gravels and sands, and built up a plain of conglomerate. Limy, shelly deposits covered the sea floor and formed layers of calcarenite, which were exposed as the sea retreated. Cliffs were formed in these deposits before a major earth movement raised them to form a high terrace, into which the rivers, adjusting to the new base-level, cut deep valleys. Since then the land has risen erratically; with the sea sometimes advancing, sometimes

Fig. 34 Vegetation establishes itself on massive screes near the deep, narrow Monastirakis gorge, cut by water along a fault-guided cleft.

Fig. 35 (*Top*) Karmi, amid wooded screes, where springs issue from the Kyrenia Range. (*Centre*) Klepini on the uppermost terrace (T1); erosion has exposed old, folded rocks beneath. (*Below*) Series of terraces (T2 and T3) above the coast (C), with hardened limestone cappings and much-eroded slopes.

retreating. This has created a series of terraces, each bounded by a cliff face, which exposes beds of gravel, sands and calcarenite. Dissection by the rivers has left a broken landscape, with steep-sided valleys and mesa-like blocks at different levels (Fig. 35 *centre* and *below*).

The present climate affects the land-use in various ways. The highest villages are generally sited where springs emerge from the limestones of the main range (Fig. 35 *top*). There the large talus slopes provide a mixture of minerals, and are often tree-covered. The higher, older, weathered terraces support a variety of crops—vegetables, fruit trees, grain, olives, and vines, often visibly 'zoned' about the village. But lower down there is little water in the deep valleys, especially in summer, and for some of the perched villages water supply is a problem. Unfortunately, the present alternating wet/dry seasons have caused a hard concrete-like crust (kafkalla) to form at the surface (p. 29), which makes cultivation difficult and limits the crops. The valley sides support herds of goats on poor scrub. Down by the present shoreline the water-table is higher, and pumps supply more intensive vegetable farming and citrus orchards.

Thus past and present influences have combined to produce a recognisably 'Mediterranean' landscape in which mountains, screes, springs, terraces, gorges and dry valleys; various soils; trees, maquis and garrigue; villages and zones of cultivation, with a road pattern adjusted to the valley systems, and the productive coastland are interdependent in many ways.

Many similar geomorphological processes have affected the wetter parts of the Mediterranean lands, though the effects of greater altitude and a more maritime location can be seen. In the Moroccan Atlas, for example, precipitation tends to increase with altitude, and, of course, air temperature decreases. During periods of glacial advance, ice eroded parts of the high Atlas and formed moraines, and rivers brought down large qualitities of debris. Thick deposits of sediment of various sizes were built up on the lower piedmont. With the onset of drying conditions, many of these acquired a calcareous crust. Here, however, the rivers continued to flow, but with a reduced load, so that they cut deep into the lower deposits. Here, too, the sea-level changes and periods of uplift have formed dissected terraces at various altitudes. The present climate does not favour the development of mature soils, and some of the best soils for farming are found on the older deposits. Today, rapid erosion has removed much of the debris from the higher slopes, so that most of their cedars have been replaced by Holm oaks on poor soils[11]; thus, once again, the landscape features are the result of processes past and present, yet, together, typical of this zone.

The combined effects of tectonic activity, sea-level fluctuations, and climatic influences can also be seen in Mediterranean regions in the other continents. The western coastland of south-west Australia is bounded

Fig. 36 Wheat growing on the calcareous soils of the dry plain of eastern central Cyprus. Periods of uplift and subsequent erosion are indicated by the gently tilted hard surfaces of the mesas and by their dissected slopes.

inland by the dissected, faulted edge of the old plateau. Limestones formed on its downthrow surface early in the Pleistocene, and on these the later advances and retreats of the ocean created immense shelly dunes, spread inland by the wind. In the present climate these pervious rocks combine with the summer aridity to stretch the limited water reserves of the few small rivers and of artesian sources deep in the limestones, for the demands of Perth and its spreading suburbs increase.

In California, earth movements have produced fault-guided valleys in the uplifted coastal range. These dry hills bear shrubby chaparral; but the wide, fault-bounded Salinas valley is open to the moist, cooling air from the ocean, and the combination of mists and sunshine suits the growing of temperate vegetables. With the help of irrigation, its deep soils are worked on a factory farming scale.

Looking Ahead

While we have looked specifically at morphogenic processes in the last few pages, it is obvious that they combine with other groups of variables outlined in Fig. 2 (I–III) to produce various types of topography and human landscape. Our systematic survey makes it possible to assess the effects of wider influences, like tourism. Stimulated by local conditions, such as the attractions of the Mediterranean climate, sea, and cultural features, tourism is capable of rapidly disrupting traditional economies, social practices, and natural landscapes alike, with both beneficial and unpleasant effects. Now that so much of each of these Mediterranean environments is man-made, a knowledge of how the many variables described in these categories I–IV act and interact must help us appreciate and anticipate the results and consequences of development.

References

[1]D. C. MONEY (1982) Arid Lands (Evans)
[2]D. C. MONEY (1978) Climate, Soils and Vegetation (UTP) p. 260
[3]A. H. STRAHLER, A. N. STRAHLER (1978) Modern Physical Geography (John Wiley)
[4]D. C. MONEY (1980) Polar Ice and Periglacial Lands (Evans)
[5]D. C. MONEY (1980) Tropical Savannas (Evans)
[6]D. E. ALEXANDER (1980) I Calanchi—Accelerated Erosion in Italy *Geography* **65** p. 95
[7]J. M. HOUSTON (1964) The Western Mediterranean World (Longman) p. 107
[8]I. G. SIMMONS (1980) Ecological-Functional Approaches to Agriculture *Geography* **65** p. 305
[9]H. BOWEN-JONES, J. C. DEWDNEY, W. B. FISHER (1961) Malta (Durham Univ.)
[10]W. DREGHORN (1971) Rocks and Scenery in the Kyrenia Region (Nicosia)
[11]H. AWAD (1963) The Geomorphology of Morocco Related to Quaternary Climate *Geog. Journ.* **129** p. 129

Other Sources

S. R. EYRE (1975) Vegetation and Soils (Arnold)
D. R. HARRIS, C. VITA-FINZI (1968) Kokkinopilos—a Greek Badland *Geog. Journ.* **134** p. 537
O. PULUNIN, A. HUXLEY (1978) Flowers of the Mediterranean (Chatto & Windus)
J. TIVY (1977) Biogeography (Oliver & Boyd)
H. WALTER (1979) Vegetation of the Earth (Springer-Verlag, New York)

Points for Discussion

1 Reasons for the unique nature of the climate of Mediterranean lands.

2 Why these lands have such a variety of small, distinct environmental regions.

3 The influences of past climates on the present soils and vegetation.

4 Reasons for vegetation similarities but floristic differences between the world's Mediterranean regions.

5 Advantages and disadvantages of occasionally burning vegetation.

6 The effects adjoining regions have on the countries about the Mediterranean and on warm-temperate south-west Australia.

7 Particularly large volumes of scree, and frequent mass movements, are associated with steep slopes in these countries.

8 The importance of recognising factors which affect soil-water fluctuations in a selected system.

9 Whether there are geomorphic features which might be described as 'typically Mediterranean'.

10 Interference with soil–vegetation systems has had many unfortunate results.

11 Men have always had to make considerable inputs to make the most of these lands.

12 Mediterranean climates seem to have favoured the early development of civilised societies.

13 Tectonic activities have had, and continue to have, a great bearing on the nature of the physical and human landscape.

14 These regions are particularly attractive to mass tourism. Yet, for various reasons, the Mediterranean itself is especially vulnerable to pollution.

15 Direct and indirect forms of energy have always been used in agriculture, but the energy requirements of various forms of rural land-use vary considerably.

16 Circumstances under which maquis may well be a climatic climax form of vegetation.

17 Various ways in which deciduous shrubs, sclerophylls, and succulents are adapted to survive the long summer drought.

Glossary

air mass a large body of air of considerable depth in which horizontal temperature and humidity gradients are relatively slight
artesian water water held in a rock which permits its passage and allows it to rise to the surface in a well
aspect direction towards which a slope faces
biotic pertaining to life
calcarenite a limestone with very small grains
calcareous containing calcium carbonate
cation (see **ion**)
cell-sap a liquid which fills parts of a plant cell cavity not occupied by protoplasm: water with solutions of many chemical substances
climax vegetation the final composition of plant communities developed from colonisation to a state of approximate equilibrium with the environment
conglomerate gravel and rounded boulders in a matrix of finer material compacted into a rock
cuticle an outer layer of leaves and stems, with cell walls almost impermeable to water
cyclonic system one in which air spins about an axis vertical to the surface
duricrust a surface or near-surface crust hardened by infiltrating solutions which leave cementing materials
ecosystem a complex integrated system in which living communities and their non-living environment interact
edaphic pertaining to the soil
erica heath plants, chiefly woody shrubs
evapo-transpiration the combined loss of water from surfaces and by transpiration from plants
floristic related to an identified and classified plant
geomorphic related to the shape of landforms
geophyte plant with bulb, tuber or rhizome well buried in the soil
herbaceous vegetation of flowering plants whose stems are not woody
humus a substance produced by the slow decomposition and oxidation of organic matter on, or near, the surface
hydrological pertaining to water, its properties and distribution
illuviated (zone) with material brought, usually in solution, from an upper horizon in the soil profile
inselberg a steep-sided, isolated hill—often a tropical residual
ion an atom, or group of atoms, positively charged through losing electrons (cation) or negatively charged through gaining electrons (anion)
karst limestone affected by severe weathering; fluted, fretted and containing shafts, caverns and pits
leaching removal of soil materials in solution by percolating water
leguminous plant of the order of Leguminosae, whose root nodules have nitrogen-fixing bacteria; it enriches the soil with nitrogen compounds
lithosphere the earth's solid rocks: often applied to the outermost rock layer
mallee vegetation dominated by small 'mallee' eucalypts, in each of which many stems arise from an underground stock
marl unconsolidated, soft mixture of calcium carbonate with clay and other impurities
micro-climate climate of shallow air layer near the ground, including soil surface and the plants
morphogenic related to the evolution of specific landforms
nitrifying conversion of nitrogen, or nitrogen compounds, to substances which can be used in biological processes
organic matter that which makes up, or is derived from, living substances
osmotic pressure that involved in the movement of solvent molecules (usually water) from a dilute to a more concentrated solution through a selectively permeable membrane
pH value a measure of the degree of acidity or alkalinity (neutral 7.0: acid smaller values, alkaline larger values)
photosynthesis the conversion of carbon dioxide and water into organic compounds by solar energy and plant chlorophyll

piedmont 'at the foot of the mountain'; often applied to general slopes away from a mountain
plutonic related to rocks formed by great heat at depth
pluvial characterised by much rain
protoplasm the fluid making up the cells of living organisms: it contains proteins
pyrophyte a plant adapted to survive the regular occurrence of fire
regolith a mantle of debris and material weathered from and covering the bedrock
sclerophyllous having organs with thickened cell walls to protect against the loss of water
scree (see **talus**)
siliceous formed of silica
soil-water water held in the *soil* and available to plants through their root systems
soil horizon a horizontal layer of variable depth with properties differing from the soil above and beneath
stomata the pores in the epidermis of plants which allow gaseous exchange to occur
sub-artesian water water held in a rock which does not flow spontaneously from a bore, but which may be pumped out
succulent a plant which stores water in its tissues
talus material weathered and detached from a rock face forming a slope beneath
tectonic related to movements of the earth's crust
transhumance a regular movement of pastoralists and stock between areas seasonally favourable for grazing
tuff rock formed from fine material thrown out by volcanic explosion
xerophytic vegetation adapted to dry environmental conditions